Amazing Noses & Terrific Tails

Steve Pollock

BBC CHILDREN'S BOOKS

Hello! I'm Jake the polar bear and this is Stinky the skunk from *The Animal Show*. Some animals have amazing noses and terrific tails that can make them look a little strange. We're going to find out why they have these noses and tails and what they use them for.

Hello, I'm Ringo the elephant. I have a tremendous trunk and I'll be telling you about all the different things I use it for.

I'm Morton the beaver and my funny-looking tail does a very special job, so I wouldn't like to be without it.

I'm Arlene the aardvark and although my nose looks very strange, it's very useful indeed when I want my dinner!

So what are noses all about, Jake?

Well, Stinky, a nose is mostly for sniffing and smelling. The strongest sense for most people is sight, but for a dog, the strongest sense is smell. All dogs have a strong sense of smell and they can pick out one particular smell from lots of others. Bloodhounds can be trained to follow smells left by individual animals and people.

▽ **Bloodhounds**

△ **Common shrew**

This shrew is a tiny animal but it also has a very strong sense of smell. As you can see, its eyes are quite small and it cannot see very well. But that long nose with all those sensitive whiskers helps it to find worms and other insects to eat, using its sense of smell.

◁ *Tapir*

So why do animals all need different sorts of noses?

Well, it depends on what kind of animal you are and the life you lead. We tapirs have a nose which looks a little like a small elephant's trunk. We like to feed on plants which grow on muddy riverbanks. Our long nose helps us to reach and grab these plants and pull off the leaves to eat them.

△ Aardvark

I'm Arlene the aardvark and I need a long nose for a different reason. I am a kind of anteater and I eat termites, which are rather like ants. Termites build nests made from mud which dries as hard as concrete. I use my strong front claws and legs to break open the termites' nests. My snout hides a great long sticky tongue which I use for lapping up the termites.

This anteater is a lot more hairy than Arlene. Those hairs help stop her from being bitten and stung by the ants. She has no teeth at all, because like the aardvark her long snout contains a sticky tongue for slurping up ants. Who needs teeth when you're eating ants?

▽ *Giant anteater and young*

As for me, I like a little bit more variety in my food and for that I use my really useful trunk. I can use it to reach leaves or fruit high up in a tree. I can use it to pull a tree up if I want to eat the whole tree. I can even pick up tiny things like peanuts with the very end of my trunk. It's great too for throwing dust all over myself to cool down, or for sucking up water and spraying it into my mouth.

Male elephant feeding on tree ▷

Proboscis monkey △

Wow, just look at that nose, Jake! Why does this monkey have a nose like that?

This is a proboscis monkey from Borneo and a prominent nose like that is helpful. It tells others in the monkey group that the one with the biggest nose is the leader. He fights off males from other groups by shouting very loudly and making a really horrible noise. His large nose helps make the noise even louder and more horrible.

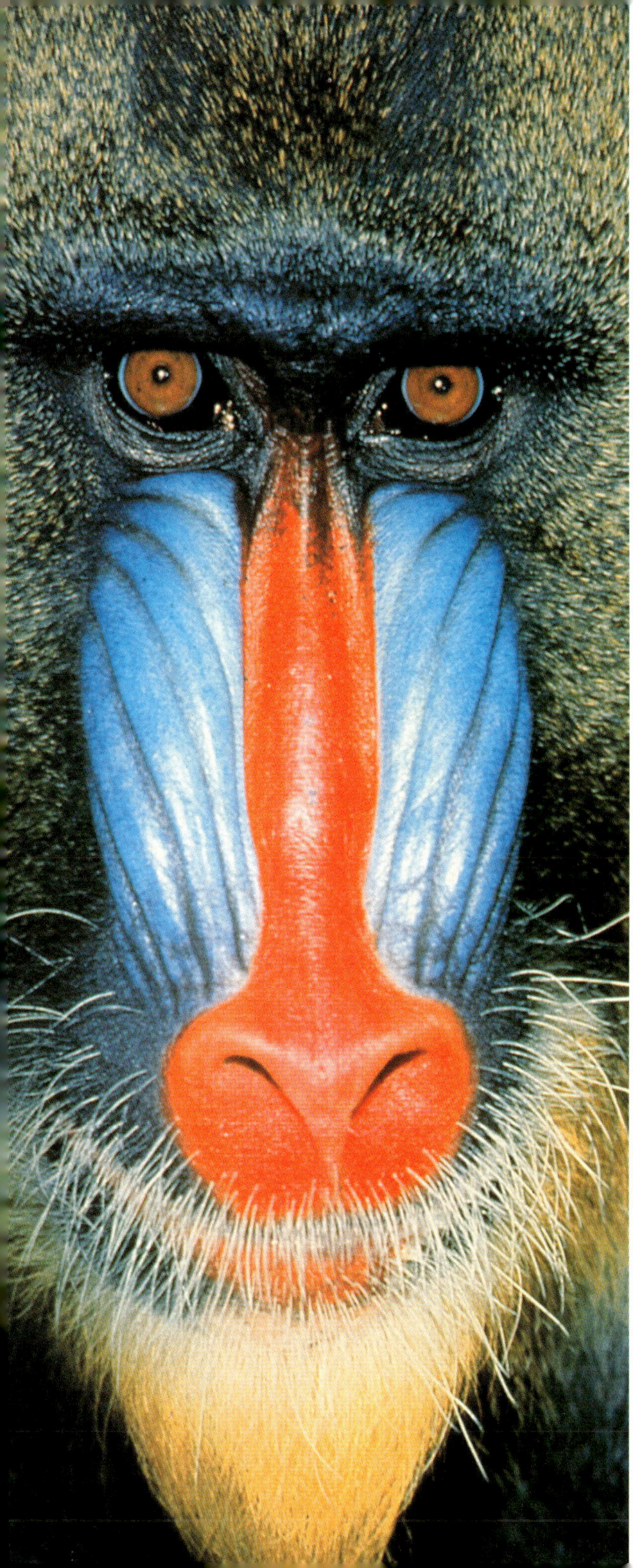

◁ *Mandrill*

This is a mandrill from Africa and the bright colours on his nose and face tell others that he is a powerful adult male. The females and younger males do not have such bright colours on their faces. A male mandrill also has bright colours on his bottom, so that any other monkey knows exactly who is boss, whichever way he's facing! So you can see that some noses and tails are used to send messages.

 **Leopard**

Here is a tail with a signal built in. The white tip of this leopard's tail can give messages to other leopards. It is very helpful for grown up leopards to wave it around so that their babies can follow them through the long grass of the African plains. Some other kinds of wild cats such as cheetahs also have white patches on the end of their tails for signalling.

The peacock puts on a spectacular show with its back feathers. They are not really its tail, but a set of special feathers which it grows to show off to females. The more wonderful the show, the more likely it is that the peacock will find his perfect lady peahen. The peacock can use its feathers to scare other males away too.

▽ *Peacock*

◁ *Striped skunk*

Tails which give out signals can be tails for protection too. Take us skunks. Just look at our lovely tails. Their black and white stripes make us stand out and they also send a warning to other animals. They are saying: "Come too close and something nasty will happen." And do you know what happens? The skunk squirts a really disgusting smell, which scares off everything. After all, who wants to eat a meal that smells like it's gone off?

△ *Pangolin*

This pangolin also uses its tail for defence. It is covered in scales like armour which protect it. The pangolin can roll up into a ball and use its tough, scaly tail to cover up the soft parts of its body underneath. That way its tail can save its life if some big animal like a leopard fancies it for breakfast.

Some animals can do amazing things with their tails. Look at this woolly monkey from South America. Its tail helps it move from tree to tree as it makes its way through the tropical forest. The tip of the tail is bare and is just like an extra finger for gripping. It's even got a kind of fingerprint, just like your fingers.

Woolly monkey △

You can see the same kind of tail on other animals. This silky anteater lives in the same part of the world as the woolly monkey and uses its tail to grip up in the trees too. It can feed on ants and termites whilst hanging upside down by its tail. Tails which are used for gripping like this are called *prehensile* tails.

▽ *Silky anteater*

Ring-tailed lemur ▷

Tails also help to keep an animal balanced. Take us lemurs for example. We live in the forests of Madagascar and when we move around in trees, we use our tail to balance. It is particularly useful when we leap from one tree and cling on to another. We also use our tail as a kind of fan. We wipe it with smells from under our arms and then wave it about. These smelly messages let other lemurs know where we are.

Red kangaroo △

Hi, I'm a kangaroo from Australia. When kangaroos hop along, the tail helps to keep us balanced as we move. We can twist and turn easily and our tail helps us to steer our way as we move. When we rest, kangaroos can lean back on their tails rather like an old man leans on a stick.

I'm a manatee and like fish, dolphins and whales, I use my powerful rounded tail to swim in rivers and coastal waters. Manatees feed on plants growing in the water or at the side of the riverbank and we have to push our heads out of the water to reach the plants growing on the bank. Some people used to think that we looked like mermaids when we did this. That is how the stories of mermaids started.

Manatee △

△ *Beaver*

Hi, I'm Morton the beaver. My tail looks as though it is used for swimming but it's my feet that do all the really hard work. I use my tail for signalling instead. When there is danger around I slap it hard against the water and it makes a really loud splash. All the rest of my family hear it and we hide away in our home until the danger has gone. It seems like a very big tail to carry around, but it can save our lives.

I had no idea that noses and tails were so important for animals, Jake.

Yes Stinky, there are so many different animals around and each one has a nose or a tail that does a special job, depending on what the animal needs it for.

Now that you've seen so many different noses and tails, see if you can work out what these pictures are. What would animals use a tail and a nose like this for? The answers are on page 24.

What do you think this is?

And this?

Answers to page 23
1. A crocodile's tail. It's used by the crocodile to swim and as a weapon for fighting attackers. You can see how powerful it looks.
2. A star-nosed mole. The strange star shape at the end of its nose helps it to feel for worms and insects underground.

Picture Credits

All wildlife photographs supplied by **Oxford Scientific Films** and credited to: **Animals Animals** page 4 (Robert Pearcey); **Anthony Bannister** page 12; **Mike Birkhead** page 13; **Martyn Colbeck** page 9; **Stan Osolinski** page 23 (top); **Partridge Productions Ltd** front cover and page 10; **Photo Researchers** pages 11 (Toni Angermayer), 17 (Jany Sauvanet), 20 (Douglas Faulkner), 21 (Leonard Lee Rue III) and 23 (bottom, Rod Planck); **Mark Pidgeon** page 18; **Wendy Shattil and Bob Rozinski** page 14; **Survival** pages 5 (Liz and Tony Bomford), 6, 7, 8 (all Alan Root), 15 (Jen and Des Bartlett), 16 (Alan Root) and 19 (Jen and Des Bartlett).

Published by BBC Children's Books
a division of BBC Worldwide Publishing
a subsidiary of BBC Worldwide Limited
Woodlands, 80 Wood Lane, London W12 0TT

First published 1996
Text and design copyright © BBC Children's Books 1996
Based on the television series *Jim Henson's Animal Show* copyright © Jim Henson Productions, Inc. 1996
Muppet character photos and illustrations copyright © 1996 Jim Henson Productions, Inc.
Jim Henson's Animal Show with Stinky and Jake logo and character names and likenesses
are trademarks of Jim Henson Productions, Inc. All rights reserved.

ISBN 0 563 40452 3

Typeset by BBC Children's Books
Cover printed by Clays Ltd, St Ives plc
Colour separations by DOT Gradations, Chelmsford
Printed and bound in Great Britain by Cambus Litho, East Kilbride